59 Prayers

Poems by

Cheryl Racanelli

Printed in the United States of America
ISBN: 978-0-692-88214-6
Library of Congress Control Number: 2018905142

Cover design by Wyndjammr Design
Cover photograph © Cheryl Racanelli
Author photograph © Jay Racanelli

Serene Artist Press

For my mother, Mary, who taught me to love.

Contents

Hello i

Butterfly Epiphany 3

I Cannot Believe in That God Anymore 4

Signs 6

A Part Irish Blessing 7

How to Pray Barefoot, Early Spring 8

Prayer for Clear Space 10

for the hungry ones 12

For Recovering One's Health 13

On Forgetting Your Camera 14

Before a Big Decision 16

Blessing for the Traveler 17

Angel of Instead 18

Before a Job Interview 19

For Getting in the Clear 20

What Mary Saw 22

M 23

Vintage Rosary 24

My Mother's Face Is Beautiful 25

One Week Later 26

Prayer for a Drinker 27

Forgiveness 28

Heart Surgery 29

Blessings 30

The Parable of Sea Glass 31

Union.. 34

The Subtlety of Protection 36

For Replenishment 37

Lapse 38

Help 39

For a Weak Day...40

For the Moment 41

While You Are Praying for Signs 42

For Taking an Exam.. 44

Prayer for Unblocking a Writer....................... 45

Blessing for Marriage 46

Miracles Will Be Involved................................47

When a Legend Dies... 48

Surrender...50

When Feeling Insignificant...............................51

Blessing on a Long Line.................................... 52

A Blessing for Healing...................................... 53

Angels.. 54

Prayer to St. Brigid for Creativity 56

Blessing for the Thing You Must Do Alone.................57

For a New Way of Being 58

Prayer for Surgery 60

I Want to See God...61

Do I Have Enough? 62

Let Changing Sheets Be a Prayer 63

In These Times 64

At Bedtime 66

For Safe Passage 67

Seventeen Lights 68

When You Need a Reason 70

Prayer for the New Year 71

For an Ordinary Day 72

Mother of All Mothers 74

For John O'Donohue 76

Finding Holy 78

Hello

First of all, dear reader, thank you for opening this book and offering me the privilege of sharing my work with you.

59 *Prayers* is a collection of poems that blossomed from the union of my writing life and my spiritual life. It is not a book of religion or sanctioned prayers. It is simply a book of poems that express my contemplation of love, doubt, suffering, and joy. My writing is drawn from the well of my spiritual experience, which includes Christianity and Buddhism. I prefer to dissolve the boundaries and let my work float where it will. The poems in this volume each started from a state of prayer, which for me is time spent opening myself to the soul's questions. Prayer is expansive, with an infinite capacity to hold whatever the human heart creates. My heart created these poems.

In an unexpected way, this volume is also a loose account of a seven-year journey. In the spring of 2010, I became seriously ill. After the initial crisis, I was left with a set of neurological anomalies and a body that could tolerate almost no exertion. My days were emptied of all work and activity. My movement was severely limited. Suddenly, I was faced with the raw reality of living a quiet, still life, housebound and too fatigued to participate in most activities.

I learned to navigate the most difficult spells, when I could do little more than lie still with my eyes closed, by writing in my head, arranging and rearranging words on the screen of my mind. Writing poetry in this space enabled me to contemplate and process my challenges and gave me a way to discover beauty and joy in the life I now had.

As a way to participate more fully in the lives of my loved ones, I began writing poems and blessings for them as they experienced life events. While I can never be sure of the effect any of the blessings had on the intended recipients, I know with certainty that prayer changes the one who prays.

Two years into my illness, after I had made a partial recovery, the statue of Our Lady of Fatima was touring New Jersey, appearing for 24 hours in each of a select group of churches, one of which was in my childhood hometown. Even though I was raised Catholic, I was unsure who Our Lady of Fatima was or why the statue was important. On top of that, I was estranged from the Catholic Church. But something in me wanted to see this statue. My mother joined me, and we sat in the church for hours, mysteriously captivated. I learned that "Our Lady of the Holy Rosary of Fatima" is a name given to Mary, the mother of Jesus, based on her appearance in 1917 to three children in Fatima, Portugal. But more importantly, visiting this sacred presence with my mother turned out to be a deeply moving, mystical experience and a gateway into a realm I could not have imagined.

Within a few months of that visit, I fell into a terrible relapse. At my mother's suggestion, we began a brief session of daily prayers together over the phone. Neither of us had ever done this before. Even though I was angry with God, I prayed anyway. It gave me an opportunity to complain out loud. Eventually, the prayers began to soften me. My heart opened to an unexpected connection to Mother Mary, a devotion that transcended boundaries and convention. I was led through prayer to experiences that have brought me healing in every aspect, including the physical.

In gratitude for answered prayers and the many miracles I have received, I chose 59 poems for this volume. In the Catholic tradition, the most familiar set of prayer beads is called a rosary, from the Latin term for "rose garden," and is strung with 59 beads. One prayer is said on each bead.

This book is a rose garden where the roses are arranged neither chronologically nor thematically. Instead, I arranged them prayerfully. I imagine you, my dear reader, ambling through the pages, finding the one rose, one bead, one poem that has meaning for you in that moment. Some of the poems flow with the cadence of traditional prayer, such as "Before a Job Interview," "Blessing for Marriage," and "Blessing for the Traveler." Other poems come from my attempt to find beauty and divinity in an imperfect world or in an imperfect life. Some come from a place of struggle or questioning, others from a sense of presence and communion. I trust that a good poem will greet you. Maybe in that poem you will find an affirmation of your own truth. Maybe you will find something to share. Or maybe you will sense a new way of being.

I could not part without telling you that 59 *Prayers* is also a testament to my mother's indestructible love for me. We still say prayers together daily. She still listens to my every lament. She still wants to hear every poem I write. I wish I had a thousand books to dedicate to her. Even that would not be enough.

As you turn this page, may you be blessed. And may you bless freely wherever you go next.

59 Prayers

Butterfly Epiphany

Without the eyelid of judgment,
Everywhere
becomes the mirror
of my own
beauty.

Nothing real stops me.
What is real
lifts me.
My two wings—
poetry and prayer—
unzip the veil.
My flight pens
a white message
briefly visible.

I Cannot Believe in That God Anymore

that giant man with a biblical beard
looming in the sky
unhappy with my mistakes
sending me bad stuff.

The God I love is a beach blanket
wild with orange and hot pink patterns
sheer enough for light and air
to drift through,
the kind of blanket
that catches in the sunny beach breeze,
flapping and bubbling,
the blanket I can't wait to
smooth across the hot sand
and plunk my goofy bones down on
so that I can soak in the full menu
of blissful beach therapies:
salt, sand, sun, sleep.

On ordinary days, like today,
when God is not a beach blanket,
she picks up her knitting
and settles down next to me on the couch
so I can take a nap without worrying.

As I lose myself in the reverie
of the God/beach blanket metaphor

and all its possibilities,
she loops her long hair behind her ear,
leans over, all pleased,
and kisses my forehead,
right on the third eye.

Signs

Seeing signs
requires intention.
I cannot tell you
what to look for.
I can only tell you
how they come to me—
as a leaf, a cloud, or anything
heart-shaped,
as an event, joyful or jarring,
a moonrise or traffic jam—
anything that feels heavy with change.
It may open like a webpage
or a book in my brain
to a passage with insight
or specific direction.

But the loveliest of signs
are those that require
no effort or translation.
They simply arrive,
transcendent reminders
of Something Divine.

A Part Irish Blessing

If I were full Irish, I could say to you,
    may your road be blessed,
and the container of these words would
    automatically hold
every highway, every turn, every tree on the side, every
    leaf on the tree.
It would cover not only pavement and gravel, but every
    flight path, railbed, waterway,
every metaphorical trail you might conceive of or
    encounter.
It would encompass all weather, all sunlight, and every
    moonrise.
It would illuminate your conversations, your daydreams,
    your calculations,
and most certainly your love.

But as I am only part Irish, I must conjure explicitly,
not so that you would know all this,
but so that my other parts might learn.

How to Pray Barefoot, Early Spring

Go to the grove of trees.
Go to the sacred grove
of the sacred trees.
Those three sturdy beings
near the stream,
or the thin twins
where you buy bread,
or the full wild forest
in your head.
If there is any question
about their sacredness,
ask.

Take off your shoes
and stand with your flesh
touching the earth,
which is surprisingly
soft and unexpectedly
warm.

Remember,
as the sweet virgin grass
awakens your soles,
what is spring,
what is eternal.

And without uttering a sound,
simply be
in the ongoing prayer
that exists among those trees,
the earth,
and the small head of grass
rising between your toes.

As you remain still
within this integrating psalm,
something in you
will inevitably heal.

Prayer for Clear Space

May I take the time this morning to fold my pajamas
    neatly.
May I wash my breakfast bowl as soon as I use it.
May I return my meditation pillow to its corner.

May I sit in a clear, clean space today,
unencumbered by clutter of the quotidian,
unburdened by the overdose of media and
    memorabilia.

May I remember that there is nothing more
    important
than what I cannot see.

May I move past stale objects that hold no promise,
past the desire for a shiny new anything,
and spend time in the vacant lot
that is missing nothing,
brimming with idea and spirit.

May I create something from the invisible.

May I leave every space today with my industry
    stowed,
my refuse discarded, my messes swept,

remembering how it first felt to enter the space
    clean,
remembering how space can be
an awakening.

for the hungry ones

how will you feed the hungry?
      will you buy bread, serve
            soup, open
                  your wallet?
      will you let a dove fly out
            and in
with messages?

whose hunger will you feed?
      will you sew your pocket hole
            or will you tear it open?
      which train goes to the people?
how will you remember their names?

For Recovering One's Health

Let me pray for these possibilities, even if
at the moment I don't believe in any of them.

    I regain my strength, and my body becomes
    lean and strong, a willowy gazelle.
    My immune system looks in the mirror and
    stops attacking what is not an invader.

    I am free from this illness.
    I gather with laughter and joy
    in my circle of friends.
    I care for those who need my care.

    I write every word I've ever longed to write.
    My hand and mind are strong.
    My daily skies abound
    with messages, blessings, and signs.

    I sing.
    I walk.
    I leap.

    I am not afraid of dying,
    neither am I afraid of living.

On Forgetting Your Camera

Today on your errands
you planned to stop at the simple park,
knowing on a rainy day
the picnic grove would be empty.
You thought you'd stop quickly,
drink your cup of coffee,
and head on to the next whatever.

The park was as you expected, quiet.
The clouds, still heavy and dark,
had wrung themselves dry hours ago,
leaving only a pleasant freshness.

What you didn't know
was that at the edge of the embankment
lay a stream you had not yet discovered,
and that before you could approach it
to further your delight,
you would spot a slender egret,
bright white against the fresh greens,
that you would stumble upon
his private tai chi practice,
watch his neck straighten to a pencil,
and curl into an uncial.

You didn't know that you would watch
a fish slipping about in the egret's beak
before disappearing down his gullet
into the greater river of life.

May you not dwell on the lost opportunity
to capture such an unexpected grace,
but instead settle your mind on the embankment,
allow only what is present at the moment
to nourish you,
and befriend the egret as if he were your angel
because, most certainly, he is.

Before a Big Decision

In this stormy stretch of winter,
as I ruminate on a pending decision,
may I see this time as a summer day,
the first day of summer, actually,
where I am the grassy field,
and my mind is the open sky,
the trees are my hair,
the rabbits my thoughts,
the birds my prayers,
and the clouds,
they are ideas and messages from God.

May the sky of my mind welcome
whatever litany of color,
whatever font or weight,
whatever edge, hard
or soft, She may send.

And me, being a clod of warm earth,
may I be ever patient with myself,
as I am only beginning to learn to read.

Blessing for the Traveler

May your travels be blessed.

May your transportation be comfortable.

May you have every essential and abundant luxury.

May your communications be in the universal
language of kindness.

May your inner light and the goodness of your
      presence
bless every person you meet, every village you visit.

May those same people and places bless you.

May all that you see and experience ignite new ideas.

May this be an adventure that will enrich your life
and your work in this world.

May you laugh well, eat well, rest well,
and return refreshed and inspired.

May you arrive safely at every destination,
especially home, where those who love you
wait in anticipation of your wondrous stories.

Angel of Instead

When you ask for help
a boulder may roll
down into your path

tempting you to curse it
and throw away your faith in prayers
but if you crouch low

you may discover
not exactly a boulder
but the Angel of Instead

tipping you off to the side,
into the berry-wild, the unmapped,
unconsidered solution.

Before a Job Interview

May you trust that all your preparation is solid.

May you be confident in all you have already done in your life.

May you be proud of who you are.

May you speak with clarity and conviction.

May authenticity and curiosity be your guides.

May your interviewer sense every possibility in you.

May this be a door to positive change.

May you be gracious no matter the outcome,

trusting that you are a light that will be genuinely
    welcomed.

For Getting in the Clear

When you dwell in the dark quadrant of despair
and the book of your life
has become some jumbled hieroglyphics
on a gray, windowless wall,
I stand for you.

I stand on the Green Lawn of a Better Day.
Barefoot, in *tadasana*, I stand for you,
like a mountain, grounded deeply in the earth,
and I breathe into my core your garbled chapter.

A violent wind
circles my head like a black wreath.
I remember my own tempest,
how unsure I was of my ability to endure,
how lost I was when my map of Right and Fair
burnt up.

I stand for you at the Crossroads of Change,
my feet firm, the howling wind of shared pain
crossing my head in every direction.

My hands lock over my heart,
inside a prayer grows wings
and takes flight,

hooks the maelstrom by the tail and trails away
until you and I are both once again
in the clear.

What Mary Saw

A few gathered on the grassy hill
with cameras and telescopes
to see a plate of darkness slide
across the full moon.
Others watched a sitcom, unaware.
This is the way with all miracles.
They happen
whether we notice them or not.

M

When you see my signature
it means you are awakening
to your life as a miracle

Vintage Rosary

Mother Mary, may this old rosary
that has come into my hands
be a blessing in my life.

I give thanks for every person who held it,
for every person who prayed on it,
for every person who passed it on.

I pray that this rosary be free
of any memory of darkness or pain,
allowing the light of its earlier work
to brighten and augment my own prayers.

May my touch upon these beads
leave a mark of beauty
to be a blessing
to the next hands that hold them.

I pray for peace.

My Mother's Face Is Beautiful

It's always been that way.
Years of love have softened her gaze,
creating an ease and an aura
that welcome me,
no matter what the weather.

My mother's face is beautiful.
And always will be so.

One Week Later

in response to the terrorist attack in Brussels, March 2016

The shock waves
have not ceased to pulse
outward from the terminal
through Brussels
across every body
of water
and every body
that reels
on this rocky planet.

We are love,
those who buffet the waves
with whispered prayers
from our faraway posts,
linking, locking,
writing a reply
immutable as the stars
and growing longer
with each new signature:
we are love, we say,
we are love, we pray,
We Are Love.

Prayer for a Drinker

Someone loves you enough to think
you drink too much.

The empty bottles you leave behind
are breadcrumbs for trouble.

The sting on your tongue
taints your best thought.

What is your best thought?

When you lift the next vessel
may you see nothing but black tar.

May you see that the bottle
is always an invitation from a stranger
to make you, drop by drop,
a stranger to yourself.

Look up at the sky tonight.
Even in the bleakest hour
there is something to discover,
even if it is only this, my prayer for you.

Forgiveness

I'm going to sit
under this tree
and say I love me
a thousand times

Under this tree of a thousand
white blossoms
I say to myself
I love me

I love me
I love me
flowering above me
a crown of white blossoms
to heal me—I love me
and light up—I love me
the night sky—I love me
that joins us together—I love me
I love me
a thousand times
I love me

Heart Surgery

When she whispered
    I am speaking through your heart
I knew she meant not to me.
She who is larger than the stars
    gave promise to shrink into my heart,
        become a mystery to solve a mystery.

Comes the day, I pray hello
    as I open the door to my heart
      and fall asleep.
The doctor enters with a lovely light
to mend a broken pathway.
She who relaxes with the angels welcomes him,
    answers his questions
until my heart is lit, and love
    radiates cleanly in every direction.

I awaken to a heart in me
    that is neither muscle nor drum,
but glowing space, a vessel
    of soft light to guide my way,
a mystery to solve a mystery.

Blessings

One long sleepless night
I counted seven thousand
and still was not done.

The Parable of Sea Glass

One summer evening, as dusk gathered on the Jersey
    shore,
Jesus turned to the kite-fliers, frisbee-throwers,
lovers, loners, and bennies,
and said,

The kingdom of heaven is like this:

At first the crowd thought he was talking about
a perfect summer night, like this one,
but he continued,

An artist made a beautiful glass globe.
He beheld its perfection for seven days.
Then he let it shatter.
Countless pieces fell
into the dark ocean like rain.
There they tumbled and tossed
in the storms and tides.

Eventually the pieces began to wash ashore,
but they were no longer clear and gleaming
with everything perfectly visible through them
from every angle.

Instead, *they were frosted and dulled,*
their original color and clarity obscured
by the crust of the ocean.
Yet,

said Jesus,

they were translucent.

A little boy digging in the sand
looked up and asked,
"What are trains losing?"

Jesus smiled.

He knelt before the boy
and pulled from behind the boy's ear
an awesome piece of sea glass
the size of a fist or a fish.

Jesus stood and held it out to the crowd, and said,
I tell you this:
hold one another up to the light
and see, then, if you have eyes.

Some in the crowd thought he was a lunatic
and wanted to beat him up under the boardwalk.
Others fell to their knees,
blinded by the brilliant light
shining through the sea glass.
For one reason or another,
they all wanted to touch him.
But by then he had given the glass to the boy
and vanished.

Union

sitting crossed-legged to meditate
I had no intention of reaching
anything sublime
but only of counting my breath
till the timer went off

then without warning
the sun beamed through me
and I was pixelated
just like on star trek

dissolved into grains
suspended in air
in the shape of me

no longer solid
but still fully there
I was filled with light and space

I was me without the heavy
pulsing veins of struggle
I was me with a hole where every
heavy thing inside me,
including the kitchen sink,
had vanished

space and light moved freely
through me, with me
as if it were divinity
and I were just my soul

The Subtlety of Protection

When you pray for protection,
    do not look for a castle
    or a sword.
Protection may arrive as a thought
    to do one microscopic action
    that seems totally unrelated
but triggers a network of happenings
    that you may never see,
a subtle web that lands you
here, in this very moment,
    safe.

For Replenishment

I know it's difficult to stop what you're doing,
but it's necessary.
Every *body* needs rest.
Yours does now.

Do not put off
the replenishment your body,
your vision, your senses, your brain,
your soul require.
All that awaits your return
will receive your better self.
Go now into the deep quiet
that is your sanctuary and source.

Lapse

The saints become silent
and the angels freeze.
Alone before dawn
I feel nothing or no one divine.
Only my broken friend, fear,
lingers like an old dog.
At times like this
whom else can I count on?

In the darkness, I am a sieve,
holding neither courage nor love.
I wrap myself in a cocoon of blankets
trying to pool what is left.

If only I could remember daybreak
and how the holy ones assemble about me,
a fluid, traveling wreath,
gently coaxing this wisp out of hiding.

Help

Without you, I would not be giving thanks
beside this golden tree.
This beautiful path,
the strength I now claim,
would be sore dreams.

When I was weak,
you were generous.
What I could not do myself,
you did for me with compassion.

What you cleaned, prepared, wrapped, carried
was really a pearl—
a thousand pearls—
and I wear them always.
How can I not?
Help received is always a gift.
And I am forever changed
by its luxury.

For a Weak Day

When you are too weak to pray,
do not pray.
Slip instead inside the empty vessel
of stillness.

Even if you are saturated with pain
and your spirit has evaporated from within,
you can float.

So float now
on the Reservoir of Every Prayer,
that pristine accumulation
of the essential human desire
for blessing.

For the Moment

Thank you for this moment,
    this very moment,
in which I have so much.

Thank you for the blessing
of remembering your love in me.

Thank you for the mountain of ideas,
the valley of imagination,
and the wild horses
of mystery and skepticism,
and for the gentle meadow of breath.

Thank you for all that is fragile in me,
and for the courage to create a prayer.

Thank you the black velvet of rest,
the constellation of angels,
and the simplicity and welcome
of returning.

While You Are Praying for Signs

While you are praying for signs,
a handful of deer rest
in the woods
just beside you.

While you face east
with the morning sun glinting through
the singing trees in a blessing onto your face,
the deer face east, too.

While you are silent in devotion,
the deer you don't even know are there
are silent, too.

Only when you are done
standing before the Holy Mother,
filling your spirit for the day,
only then as you take your first step
back into your day
do you see

two deer resting peacefully
in the little valley beside you,

and between you and the deer
is your dog,
also quiet on the autumn earth.

Here you all are
in a rare harmony.

You struggle in your flawed capacity
to take in the fullness
of what you know must be
a gift.

It is not the hidden deer,
which you now discover to be five,
or the silence of your dog in their presence,
but the calm energy
that flows freely
like script
among all of you,
evenly creatures
receiving
an answer.

For Taking an Exam

May all you already know come back to you easily.
If you stumble over something unfamiliar,
may you calmly decode it in part or in full,
and sculpt an answer from what feels impossibly
    formless.
May your mind be full of light,
and all its doors and windows open,
your thoughts flowing freely through all the rooms
like a breeze.
May all your preparation yield a calm demeanor,
and may you approach every question with
    confidence.
May you pace evenly through the exam.
If you linger or are troubled,
breathe deeply and allow yourself the uncertainty,
then move on with renewed confidence in your
    ability
to solve what remains.
May your grade be fair.
May you be satisfied with your commitment to the
    course,
with your preparation for this exam,
and, therefore, be at peace with the grade you
    receive.

Prayer for Unblocking a Writer

May you toss the rock of indecision from your path.
And when you discover that underneath it lies
the rock of perfectionism,
ditch that rock, too.

Then you will see that these rocks have been
    covering
the dark pit of fear.
Lean over the pit and stare deeply.

Then pick that pit up
and see how small it is, and light,
a beechnut, actually,
that you can bury in yon field
where it will rejigger itself
into the kind of tree from which
the first books were hewn,
the thick etymological root
of the word *book*.

Blessing for Marriage

May your union be blessed.

May you each build inside yourself a sanctuary
for the other,
a safe and loving haven.

May your love be the canopy of summer trees
that offers beauty, sunlight, and birdsong
to your time together.

May you adorn each other with the jewels
of kindness, tenderness, and compassion.

May your love bless the space around you,
your home, your work, your cherished gatherings,
and every casual interaction,
because the world needs your love.

May you walk this earth together,
creating with each footstep
your beautiful and always new life together.

May your marriage be blessed.

Miracles Will Be Involved

Whatever it is you are struggling with today,
miracles will be involved.
Whatever mine you are digging in,
miracles will be involved.
Whatever stillness you are resisting,
miracles will be involved.

You forget that the rain seeps into the earth
and nourishes in ways you do not see.

Whatever you touch or say after reading this
      message,
remember that miracles will be involved.

When a Legend Dies

You want to tell everyone who didn't know him.

No, wait, to be honest,
first you dissolve into tears.
You read the online post over and over
because maybe you misread something.
You have been following his rising star
and you cannot believe it is not him writing this time
but someone who loved him
telling you he died in an accident
on a mountain in Africa
with his wife
at age 33.

You cannot believe.

You wait for him to post another video.

Meantime, you go back and reread
your favorite articles on his website,
and you hear his voice, the charm
and you cry again

because he was so young
because he was making the world better
because he made you better

without ever knowing.

You wonder how you can feel a passing so sharply
for someone you only wish you could have met
someday.

He did work that mattered
and he wrote in clear steps
how you could, too,
how you could do work that matters
how you could Live Your Legend.

You cannot stop thinking how you loved
his raw language
his unabashed idealism
his unrelenting message of possibility
his unbridled love of life.
You want to tell everyone who didn't know him.

You want to tell everyone who didn't know him
because somehow now you are his voice.

In memory of Scott Dinsmore, creator of
Live Your Legend.

Surrender

Some days there is no god.
Instead of wrestling with him,
and having to decide who won,
I just surrender.
Not to god, no.
It's the whole idea of a god
I give up.
In the emptiness I breathe
freely, with relief,
until I see at twilight a setting crescent moon
with the ghost of its full circle
luminescent on an indigo screen.
Then I find myself wondering
whom to thank.

When Feeling Insignificant

Remember, Dear One, that you are a star
and you cannot help but send
little packets of starlight
out into the dark wilderness.

Without uttering a word
or buttoning a shirt
you are shining.

Only when you shroud yourself with fear
is your light concealed.

Be free then, Dear Star, be light
and trust that the beauty and goodness
you offer by nature
is by another eye fully seen.

Blessing on a Long Line

May I take a deep breath
and be assured that no matter how fast
any other line is moving,
I am in the right line.

Bless the cashier.
May the intentions of his heart be heard by God.
Bless the person in front of me.
May her concerns be lightened.
Bless the person behind me.
May she know financial abundance.

May I be grateful for what I am about to buy
and for every luxury I can afford.
May everything I purchase
nourish or safeguard someone
and help me live like a flower or a bird.

A Blessing for Healing

May you be healed.
May your body find balance.
May your energy return.
May whatever you carry
that is not truly yours
    dissolve.
May health blossom in all the cleared spaces.
May you be peaceful and patient
while Divine Medicine and all its tributaries
    rise and flush,
    clear and nourish,
    restore and heal
every system, cell, and space,
physical and infinite.
May your breath be easy.
May your path be light.
May your song be joy.

Angels

It is difficult to believe
in angels
but I am learning.

I have often said
of my closest calls
that there was nothing
between me and death
but an angel.

Then I would return
to my quiet illusion
of self-sufficiency.

I imagine there are thousands
of rescues that were performed
for me
and I thanked no one
because I did not even feel it
I just got to where I was going.

One day I needed help
and I simply asked
do I have a Guardian One
really, or is that just in a museum painting.

I do.

An angel
radiant, shapeshifting,
strong enough to hoist a steel bridge,
soft enough to sing with snow,
light enough to recline
on a flower petal,
waiting
for my next call,
close or otherwise.

Prayer to St. Brigid for Creativity

Just as you led the Celtic mind
out to the meadow of transfiguring light,
lead also my hopeful imagination
out into a new meadow this day.

Just as you shed physical beauty for the gifts of spirit,
quell also my accumulating nature
so that the gifts of the grassy fields
may come gently into focus.

Just as you wove reeds into a tale of conversion,
may I also weave available stalks into an artful
      message.

May I be in your vein both brave and creative.

Blessing for the Thing You Must Do Alone

When you must cross a threshold that frightens you
to enter a territory you would much prefer to avoid,
may you tether to your wrist
a flock of helium balloons.
As you go where you must,
they will babble overhead
on their long threads,
following you so eagerly,
as if they were new thoughts—
ones of hope, creativity, courage
and love—
waiting, just waiting
for you to think them.

Who can maintain gravity
while holding the potential
to defy it?

Go, then, trailing the colors
of illumination, armed
with new thoughts
to lift you.

For a New Way of Being

On this day, the people will begin
to remember their humanity.
They will search for the Self
that matters, a Self unconcerned
with accumulation
of anything that does not
raise the spirit,
a Self that reflects a wisdom
not available
in the media or marketplace.

Look into their faces
and pray for their remembering
and their healing.
Then find a new place
where your own remembering
can unfold,
because that is who you were really
dreaming and praying for.
There is no other
to hate or heal.

Love yourself
for wanting to change, wanting
to help, wanting to hope,
for believing in harmony
and kindness.

Watch courage spring up
like wildflowers
along the better road.
Gather what you need,
and bring to the dark edges
of charred thought
the wild, rippling color of change.

Prayer for Surgery

May you be peaceful today.
May you go about your daily routine
and required tasks with ease.
May any preparation be simple.

May you sense your guardian angel,
and may her presence be clear to you
in the moments before surgery
reassuring you that you are watched over.

May the surgeon's work be an expression
of God's tender care.
May every hand that touches you be filled
with kindness and compassion.
May you be a light and a blessing
to those who care for you.

May the angels of healing flow in and through your
    body,
assisting your body with its healing work.
May your recovery be natural and fluent,
like floating on a calm morning ocean
with the early sunlight glinting on the water.

I Want to See God

At dusk I find her
in the deep purple cavern
of an iris bloom.

Do I Have Enough?

Did I wake up today with a blanket upon me?
Was I able to shower and wash my own body?
Did I have a choice of shirts to wear?
Do I have a habitual time for eating?

Did I notice the weather today?
Did I remember one person in prayer?
Was someone's kindness present in my day?
Was my own kindness present in someone else's day?

Was I silent enough to hear the calling of my soul?
Did I find joy in one thing?

Let Changing Sheets Be a Prayer

If you are able to change
your own sheets
consider it a blessing.
It means you have working limbs
and enough energy and health
to do this important thing.

It also means you have a bed.
Something else to be grateful for.

There is a woman who comes
to the retreat center
after the weekend
to change all the sheets.
She chooses to do this
without pay or praise.
She simply readies the bed
for the next weary
seeker of wisdom or refuge.
She rolls up the old worries
and spreads out a fresh canvas,
her arms raising and lowering,
creating a billowing ripple
in the fabric of the world,
a prayer that somehow
reaches each of us breathing.

In These Times

after the terrorist events in Orlando, Florida,
June 2016

You have turned to me
in disbelief, shaken
as the earth cracks
like bone
under the plan and force
of stricken minds.

How, you ask,
can this continue to happen?
How, you wonder,
can your tiny prayer matter?

I tell you now
that it does.
That all the tiny prayers
of the world
add up
like the grains of sand
that line the oceans.

Imagine yourself
on the shore of Holy Presence.
Release the answers
you have disguised as prayer.

Receive the messages of love
that arrive on soft waves.

Do not neglect such imagining.
It is prayer.

Walk now, back into your
day which is no longer ordinary,
and *be a sanctuary.*
Serve love.
Welcome love.
Remain in love.

At Bedtime

When evening comes, may I be grateful
for the jar of blessings that has been this day.

As the kind angel of night comes to seal the jar,
may I behold one more time through the glass
all the pearls of goodness and mercy therein,
and may I appreciate the beauty of this unrepeatable
    arrangement.

May I pull the soft blanket of night upon me
and settle into the feather bed of darkness
where nothing is demanded, nothing is due.

May I release into the hands of my angel
all ideas and worries and lists,
and let her hold for me all these until tomorrow
when I can train my refreshed attention upon them.

May I find in the emptiness and silence pure rest and
    restoration
and a time for the wisdom of my body
to do its healing work.

May my dreams be gentle as sunlight filtered through
    soft summer leaves.
May my angel keep one hand upon my heart and the
    other upon my crown,
that I may be completely secure and completely free.

For Safe Passage

when you lose yourself in a dark channel
and the ladder of gratitude has too many rungs
choose one small good thing
and let it bless you

one thing, like a leaf, a pen, a toe

thank that toe for balancing you since the day you
    learned to walk
for wearing ridiculous party colors in the summer
for being blissfully unaware of your inner despair

thank the leaf for its green soothing drink
for the filtered molecules you breathe
for the radiating veins that sketch a map for you to
    follow

thank the pen for being simple and light
for being present and ready with ink
when you have, as all travelers of darkness do,
an urgent river of expression

and be thankful as the current of that blue river
carries you through the harrowing channel, out—
out
into the bright calm space
of a waiting new page

Seventeen Lights

For the victims of the Parkland, Florida massacre,
February 14, 2018

Young Lights, shot
like stars from the firm earth,
your departure blackens
the continent.

Young Lights, who
will wear your sneakers?
who could possibly invoke
your exact brand of joy?
Young Lights, who
is beside you now?
who is beside those bending
into the blank space of loss?

Young Lights, constellate
now in the brain
of any leader too feeble
to calculate the true equations
of guns and minds and money.

Young Lights, baptize
with fire the heart of any leader

who responds to massacre
with thin sympathy
and changes nothing.

Young Lights, remember us,
forgive us,
illuminate us
as you gather at the edge
of Love's shore,
welcomed.

When You Need a Reason

It's easy to say
things happen for a reason
when the thing that is happening
is merely inconvenient
or is not happening directly to you.

Be careful when you offer the words
things happen for a reason
as wisdom or consolation to another human being.
Better to utter the words silently as a prayer
of surrender and acceptance.

Things may happen for a reason,
but not necessarily
for one that is palatable
or even discernible.

Things happen as a river happens:
each bead of water following another,
collectively carrying
all that needs to be carried
to sea.

Prayer for the New Year

May I remember to do one kind thing.
May I be grateful for all the people to whom I can say
    I love you
May I say
    I love you
to at least one of them.
May I also remember to say it to myself.
May I do these things today
and on days I forget about this prayer.

May I seek out something yellow
in any configuration.
Even if it is a yellow stripe on the spine
of a thin volume of poetry,
may I consider its contribution to the spine, the
    poetry,
and my heart,
because I'm about to leaf through the volume
and stumble upon my new favorite poem.

For an Ordinary Day

Thank you for noticing
the ordinary day,
how the sun was shining
and everything
flowed
like the little brook
you stopped to watch

how your sweet dog,
old as she is,
barely wanted to walk
up the hill
and then trotted like a pony
back down

how you made plans
for the day
and some of them worked out

how you reclined in the sun
and read a novel instead

how a dinner of spinach
and potatoes tastes
like a celebration
when made by someone
who loves you

and how your heart turned
toward the one you love
as the evening grew bright
with the crescendo of crickets
heralding change
still masked
in these last green
days of August

Mother of All Mothers

Curled over the globe of her belly,
Mary, the chosen rose,
embraces the glow of miracle,
the secret every mother carries:
there is no conception without God.

Lit from within,
her belly holds more than a child
or a king or a savior.
Mary, pearl of God's favor,
sees generations of children
arriving on the crimson rivers of time.
Without words or signs,
she senses she will be Mother of all mothers.

In darkness, she caresses
the blessed orb of her body.
With each stroke, the brilliance of her love radiates
further down the continuum of mothers,
all the way down to me,
so that here and now,
I receive her blessing.

It will take me a lifetime
to decipher the miracles and wisdom,
but I do it this way:
petal by petal,
pearl by pearl,
edging ever closer to the Mystery.

For John O'Donohue

With the nimble hand
of your words
you have
pared my sadness
like a fruit
and served
back to me
a sweetness
hidden

I want not to mourn
the words you didn't write
but to perpetuate
the teeming tides
of your wisdom

I want the waters
of your words to rain inland
upon the people dying
in the parched regions
of their heart
so they may come
to love and study
life from your window

From your window
my imperfection shrinks:

a river rushes

a meadow ripples

a willow sways

I ride on the kind wing of imagination

to the farthest coves

the sweetest valleys

the softest branches

the bluest stones

and there, the angels of beauty

invite me

and there, truth begins to unravel

melodious, mysterious,

unwieldy, divine.

Finding Holy

You have the power to bless,
to create a sanctuary anywhere,
simply by observing with reverence
     a detail
and longing to make it last

About the Author

Cheryl Racanelli began writing in third grade when she was first introduced to the magic of creative writing. After earning a technical undergraduate degree, Cheryl earned a master's degree in creative writing. Her poems have appeared in literary journals and anthologies.

Cheryl teaches free-verse poetry writing to elementary school students, and offers a companion workshop for teachers. She also leads creativity workshops for adults. Learn more by visiting www.CherylRacanelli.com.

Made in the USA
San Bernardino, CA
12 December 2019

61343600R00053